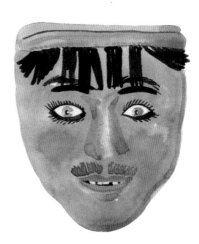

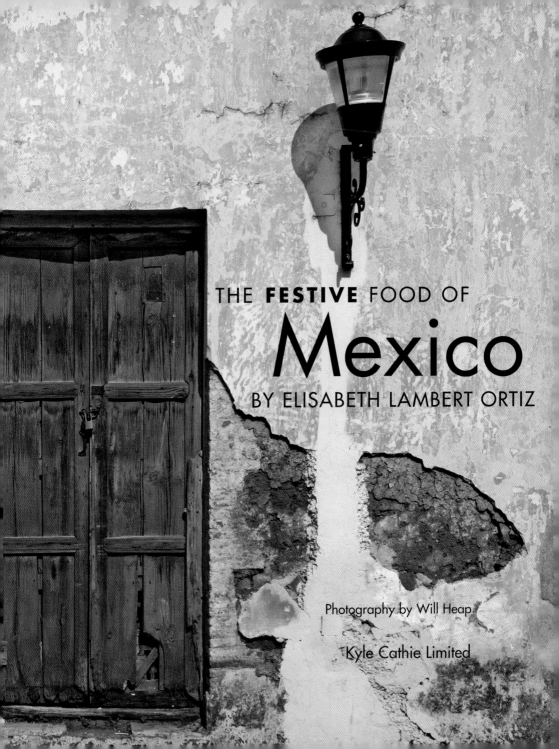

THE **FESTIVE** FOOD OF

Mexico

BY ELISABETH LAMBERT ORTIZ

Photography by Will Heap

Kyle Cathie Limited

First published in Great Britain in 1992 by
Kyle Cathie Limited
122 Arlington Road
London NW1 7HP
general.enquiries@kyle-cathie.com
www.kylecathie.com

ISBN 1 85626 629 X
ISBN (13-digit) 978 1 85626 629 1

pages 5–6: A street in San Cristobal de las Casas in Chiapas, Mexico;
Thom Lang/Corbis
pages 7–8: Cowboy; Hugh Sitton/zefa/Corbis

Designed by **pinkstripedesign.com**

Photography by **Will Heap**

Illustrations by **Sally Maltby**

Home economy by **Lizzie Harris**

Styling by **Roisin Nield**

Production by **Sha Huxtable & Alice Holloway**

A Cataloguing in Publication record for this title is available from the
British Library.

Reproduction by Colourscan Pty Ltd
Printed and bound in China by SNP Leefung Printers Limited

CONTENTS

NEW YEAR'S EVE

There are no special dishes for New Year's Eve though it is celebrated with enthusiasm. There are private parties and many people go to restaurants where they have their favourite dishes and stay up much later than usual, in fact until the Old Year dies and the New Year is born. In addition to lavish food there will be a great variety of drinks, including tequila, wine and Mexico's excellent beers. Toasts to the New Year and wishes of *Feliz Año Nuevo*, happy New Year, to friends and relations are made in champagne or a special favourite, sparkling cider, until finally the revellers get to bed, tired but happy.

The following day sees Menudo Estilo Sonora come into its own as a lifesaver after a too late, over-indulgent night. Served for breakfast whenever that may be, it is wonderfully restorative. Like a pot-au-feu, it is both soup and meat.

When served to help the hangover sufferer, traditional wisdom advises a generous helping of the crumbled chile péquin, small hot dried red chillies, served with the dish. If hominy, large white corn kernels, are not available, frozen corn kernels are the best substitute.

TRIPE SOUP SONORA-STYLE

900g honeycomb tripe
2 pig's feet, halved
1 bunch of spring onions, trimmed and chopped, using some of the green part
450g tinned hominy, or frozen whole corn kernels
50g chopped fresh coriander leaves

fresh oregano, chopped, or dried oregano, crumbled
dried péquin chillies (dried red), crumbled
1 large (Bermuda or Spanish) onion, finely chopped
6 lime or lemon wedges
salt and freshly ground black pepper

serves 6

1 Put the tripe and pig's feet into a large saucepan with salted water to cover. Bring to a simmer and cook, covered, over a low heat until the meats are tender, about 3 hours. Check the tripe from time to time and remove it as soon as it is tender. Tripe is precooked and exact cooking time is difficult to assess.

2 Cool the meats in the stock. Lift out the tripe and cut it into squares or strips. Remove the bones from the pig's feet and cut into pieces. Return the meats to the stock.

3 Add the spring onions, corn, coriander and salt and pepper to taste. Simmer over a low heat for 5 minutes.

4 Serve in deep soup bowls, with small bowls of oregano, chillies and onions, and the lime or lemon wedges on the side; add to the soup according to taste.

DÍA DE LOS REYES

KING'S DAY

This is 6th January, Twelfth Night, Epiphany, the day when the Three Kings came to visit Jesus with their gifts and is the traditional day in Mexico for children to receive their Christmas gifts. Having found out about Santa Claus many of them expect presents on Christmas Day as well but they can be sure of getting a gift on King's Day. This is the day when the Rosca de Reyes is baked. This is a ring-shaped yeast bread decorated with candied fruits and sugar and with a tiny china doll, representing the infant Jesus, baked in it. Whoever gets the china doll must give a party on 2nd February, Candlemas Day, the day of godparents.

right Mexican actors representing The Three Kings in Alameda Park, Mexico City on Janurary 5th; Reuters/Corbis

ROSCA DE REYES

KING'S DAY RING

3 teaspoons active dry yeast
1 teaspoon sugar
50ml lukewarm water
275g plain flour
½ teaspoon salt
50g sugar
2 large eggs, well beaten
4 large egg yolks
100g butter, softened
grated rind of 1 lemon
225g mixed chopped candied
  fruits and peels
1 small china doll
100g icing sugar
2 tablespoons cream
maraschino cherries, halved

1 In a small bowl prove the yeast with the sugar and water for 15 minutes or until foamy.

2 In a large bowl mix half the flour with the salt, sugar, eggs, egg yolks, butter, grated lemon rind, yeast and water and beat until the mixture is well blended.

3 Dust two thirds of the candied fruits and peels with flour and add to the mixture. Add the remaining flour and mix to a soft dough. If it is sticky, add a little more flour. Turn onto a lightly floured board and knead until it is smooth and satiny, about 5 minutes. Shape into a ring, tucking the china doll into the dough.

4 Place on a greased baking tray, put an egg cup or 10cm jar in the centre of the ring to keep it open, cover with a cloth and leave in a warm, draught-free place to double in bulk, about 2 hours. Brush the ring with melted butter and bake in a preheated oven, 180°C/350°F/gas 4, for 30 minutes, cool and transfer to a flat serving platter. Mix the icing sugar with the cream and spread over the ring. Decorate with the remaining fruits and candied peel and the halved cherries.

TAMALADA

Any excuse will serve for a festive *tamalada* – a birthday, an engagement, a family reunion – the only essential being to have someone who makes really splendid tamales. My husband's grandmother was famous for her *tamaladas*, and would co-opt neighbours to help in the three-day cooking effort. The party would be held in her garden, which was a large one, with tables and chairs set out for guests, long tables loaded with plates of tamales, salads, fruit and sweetmeats, jugs of soft drinks, bottles of tequila with bowls of quartered limes, beer and wine. Perhaps there would be music, as well as lively talk and a great consumption of tamales with many different fillings. As soon as one platter was finished, another would arrive from the kitchen to disappear with equal speed. 'Blind' Tamales, that is unstuffed ones, are often eaten as bread and in some households where a very light supper, *merienda*, is the evening meal, they may be eaten with either of the corn drinks, Atole or Champurrado. They sometimes accompany Mole Poblano but more often leftover mole is used as a filling. For dessert there are sweet tamales such as Emperor Moctezuma's favourite, stuffed with fresh strawberries sweetened with honey.

TAMALES

12–24 dried cornhusks
75g lard, softened
275g masa harina (flour for
   corn tortillas)
1½ teaspoons baking powder
1½ teaspoons salt
350ml warm chicken stock

makes 12

1 If the cornhusks are very small, double them up. If cornhusks are not available use 20 x 10cm sheets of aluminium foil topped with pieces of greaseproof paper. Soak the cornhusks in hot water until softened.

2 In a bowl cream the lard until it is very light and fluffy. Mix the masa harina with the baking powder and salt and beat in the lard bit by bit. Gradually beat in the stock, a little at a time, to make a mushy dough. To test whether the dough is ready drop a little into a glass of cold water. It should float. If it sinks to the bottom and disintegrates it needs more beating. Continue to beat until the dough is light enough to float.

3 Shake excess water from the cornhusks. Spread 1 tablespoon of the dough on the centre of each husk, leaving enough room to fold over the ends at top and bottom. Place 1 tablespoon of filling at the centre of the dough. Fold the cornhusk over so that the filling is completely covered by the dough. Fold the ends of the husks over at top and bottom and place, bottom ends down, in a steamer, and steam for about 1 hour, or until the dough comes away from the husks. If you're using foil and greaseproof paper, twist the ends to make the package watertight. Eat the tamales hot.

FOR THE FILLINGS

Tamales may be filled with a variety of fish, poultry or meats and different sauces. Leftover Mole Poblano made with either turkey or chicken is a popular filling. Sometimes there is leftover mole sauce and this can be used with cooked, shredded pork or any poultry. Enchilada Sauce (see page 32) can be used if the cream is left out. The filling for Empanadas de Vigilia (see page 40) makes a good one for tamales, so does Picadillo (see page 21) with a little tomato sauce.

left StockFood Creative/Getty Images

Picadillo

MINCED BEEF

2 tablespoons olive oil
450g lean beef mince
1 onion, finely chopped
1 garlic clove, chopped
1 tart apple, peeled,
  cored and chopped
225g tomatoes, peeled
  and chopped
2 fresh hot green
  chillies, deseeded
  and chopped
40g seedless raisins

12 pimiento-stuffed
  olives, halved
pinch of dried thyme
pinch of dried oregano
25g flaked almonds
salt and freshly ground
  black pepper

serves 6 as a main
course if the quantities
are doubled

1 Heat the oil in a heavy frying pan and brown the beef over a moderate heat. Add the onion and garlic and cook until the onion is browned. Add the apple, tomatoes, chillies, raisins, olives, thyme, oregano and salt and pepper, stir to mix and cook, uncovered, for about 20 minutes.

2 Fry the almonds in a little olive oil until they are golden, and sprinkle on top of the Picadillo. Cook for a few minutes longer if there is much liquid. The hash should be quite dry.

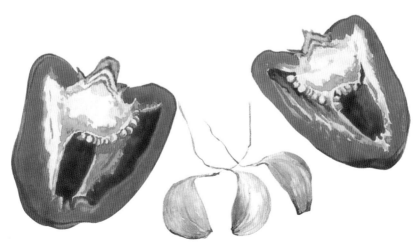

Salsa de Adobo

ADOBO SAUCE

In Spain adobo is a pickle sauce. In Mexico it is a thick chilli marinade which usually contains a little vinegar. If Mexican guajillo chillies are unobtainable, substitute crumbled dried chillies.

6 dried ancho peppers, or
  use 6 fresh red peppers
6 garlic cloves
¼ teaspoon ground black
  pepper
1 dried bay leaf, crumbled
pinch of ground cumin
½ teaspoon dried oregano
½ teaspoon dried thyme
2 tablespoons guajillo
  chillies or crumbled dried
  chillies
50ml cider vinegar

makes about 225ml

1 If using dried ancho peppers remove the stems, shake out the seeds, tear up roughly and soak in warm water for 20 minutes. Drain and purée in a food processor or blender with the garlic.

2 If using fresh peppers, remove the stems and seeds, chop and reduce to a purée with the garlic cloves. Add the pepper, bay leaf, cumin, oregano and thyme, a little of the soaking water from the dried peppers, and the chillies and reduce to a thick purée.

3 If using the sauce for main courses, stir in the vinegar and pour into a glass jar. It will keep, refrigerated, for several weeks. If using it as a sauce with tamales, heat 2 tablespoons of vegetable oil in a frying pan and sauté the mixture, stirring constantly, over moderate heat for 5 minutes. Cool. Stuff the tamales with 1 tablespoon of shredded chicken, pork or fish or whatever is being used, then top with 2 teaspoons of the adobo sauce. Steam the tamales in the usual way.

TAMAL DE OAXACA

OAXACAN-STYLE TAMALES

Instead of cornhusks, banana leaves are used for these tamales. The banana leaves are softened in boiling water and trimmed into squares. The tamales are flat and square and have a subtle but distinct flavour from the leaves. A special chilli from the region, *chile chilhuacle*, is used to make Mole Negro which like Mole Poblano contains a little unsweetened chocolate and is the special mole dish of this semi-tropical region.

TO MAKE TAMALES DE PUERCO EN SALSA DE TOMATE VERDE
Pork Tamales in Green Tomato Sauce

Have ready pork loin cooked and shredded. Combine it with Salsa de Tomate Verde (see page 24) and use as a filling for tamales.

SALSA DE TOMATE VERDE

GREEN TOMATO SAUCE

The green tomatoes in this sauce are not ordinary, unripe tomatoes. They are the fruits of *Physalis ixocarpa* and have a number of names including husk tomato which refers to their loose brown papery outer covering. The Aztecs called them *miltomatl*; they are also called *tomatitto* and less frequently *fresadilla*. Probably the most used name is *tomatillo* (little tomato). They have a unique flavour which characterised the cooking of the Aztec and Maya empires. They are available tinned and are increasingly available fresh. If used fresh they should not be peeled as nothing would be left of them but tiny seeds! They make a wonderful sauce for tamales and enchiladas, in fact they go with any Mexican dish. Taste the liquid in the tin before adding it to the sauce as it may be salty.

2 x 450g tins Mexican green tomatoes
1 medium onion, finely chopped
1 garlic clove, chopped
1–2 fresh hot green chillies, deseeded and chopped
120ml fresh coriander leaves, chopped
2 tablespoons vegetable oil
salt

1 In a food processor or blender combine all the ingredients except the oil and reduce to a purée. Add a little of the liquid from the tinned tomatoes if necessary. Heat the oil in a frying pan, add the purée and cook, stirring, over a moderate heat until it is slightly thickened. Season to taste with salt. Use with any savoury tamal.

SWEET TAMALES

1 Make a recipe for plain tamales (page 19) but reduce the salt to
½ teaspoon. (Use the chicken stock even though the tamales are sweet –
between 125g and 225g granulated sugar to the masa harina
according to taste.)

2 Prepare the cornhusks and spread with a layer of dough. Top with
1 tablespoon of combined seedless raisins, slivered almonds and
chopped citron for each tamal. Roll up and steam. Eat hot. Instead of
almonds, pine nuts can be used and the tamales can also be filled with
a mixture of chopped candied fruits such as pineapple, apricots, cherries
or peaches. Some cooks like to colour the sweet tamal light pink, in
which case mix 1½ tablespoons of grenadine syrup into the dough.

FIESTA DE LA CANDELARIA

CANDLEMAS DAY

2nd February is the day when whoever has found the doll figurine in the King's Day Ring must reciprocate with a party. It is also known as the day of the *padrinos*, godparents' day, and marks the real end of the Christmas festivities. The foods served are tamales stuffed with pork in a green chilli sauce and a special, very old Mexican drink, Champurrado, Chocolate Atole. Father Sahagún, a Spanish priest in Mexico at the time of the Conquest, mentions women being given atole, a corn gruel, at a banquet of Aztec merchants when the men were drinking chocolate, a drink forbidden to women. Champurrado is a colonial drink, a compromise as women were allowed it despite the fact that it was based on chocolate. Masa harina, the special corn (maize) meal that is used to make tortillas, is the thickening agent.

left Mexican catholics carrrying figures of baby Jesus during Mass in Mexico City in celebration of Candelaria Day; Daniel Aguilar/Reuters/Corbis

CHAMPURRADO

CHOCOLATE ATOLE

100g masa harina
   (tortilla flour)
700ml water
small piece cinnamon stick
   or 1 vanilla bean
225g light brown sugar
700ml milk
75g unsweetened chocolate,
   grated

serves 4–6

1 Combine the masa harina and water in a saucepan and stir to mix. Add the cinnamon stick or vanilla bean and cook over a low heat, stirring constantly, until the liquid has thickened.

2 Remove from the heat and add the sugar, milk and chocolate, stirring to mix. Discard the cinnamon stick or vanilla. Return the mixture to the heat and bring to a simmer. Serve hot in small cups or mugs.

VIERNES DE DOLORES

FRIDAY OF THE SEVEN SORROWS

During Lent, on the Friday before Good Friday, there is a fiesta the origins of which go back a long way. Called Friday of Sorrow or Friday of the Virgin of the Seven Sorrows, it was once a favourite fiesta of artists and writers who came early in the morning to eat tamales and drink atole for breakfast. It was also a *charro* festival with traditionally dressed horsemen, who came accompanied by girls dressed as the China Poblana, also on horseback; all immensely colourful. More recently the festival has been at the floating gardens of Xochimilco just outside Mexico City. The ancient city of Tenochtitlán was built on a lake with canals and artificial islands. Xochimilco is all that survives. Called the Venice of Mexico, it is extremely popular and somehow this sad day has become identified with a brilliant and happy fiesta where there are prizes for the best decorated boat taking people through the canals, for the best typical dancers, the best typical costume, the best singer, best guitar player and so on. Everything is decked with flowers, especially carnations and the festival ends at the village of Santa Anita, where the revellers will eat a breakfast of enchiladas or hot tamales with atole or Champurrado. Sorrow seems to have been forgotten.

left Xochimilco, Mexico City; Gala Narezo/The Image Bank/Getty Images

ENCHILADAS ROJAS CON QUESO

TORTILLAS STUFFED WITH CHEESE

1 onion, finely chopped
1 garlic clove, chopped
2 fresh hot green chillies, or
    more, seeded, chopped
700g tomatoes,
    peeled and chopped
salt
pinch of sugar
2 tablespoons vegetable oil
225ml sour or double cream

serves 4

1 To make the enchilada sauce, in a food processor, combine the onion, garlic, chillies, tomatoes, salt and sugar and purée.

2 In a large frying pan, heat the oil and pour in the purée. Cook, stirring, over a moderate heat until the sauce is thick and well blended, about 5 minutes. Cool the sauce, then stir in the cream. Set aside.

To assemble the dish, have ready:
oil for frying
12 tortillas
225g grated Cheshire or mild Cheddar
    cheese (Mexicans will use *queso de Chichuahua*)
1 onion, finely chopped

1 In a large frying pan heat the oil and fry the tortillas, one by one, for about 30 seconds on each side. Drain on kitchen paper. Warm the sauce but do not boil as it will curdle. Dip the tortillas one by one in the sauce then fill with cheese and top with onion. Leave enough cheese and onion for the garnish.

2 Roll up the tortillas and put them into an ovenproof dish. Pour the remaining sauce over the tortillas, sprinkle with the remaining cheese and onion and put the dish into a preheated oven, 180°C/350°F/ gas 4, for about 10 minutes to heat through. Serve as soon as possible as enchiladas go soggy if left to stand.

These enchiladas can be served on fast days. Another suitable stuffing would be scrambled eggs, about 6 for 12 tortillas. On non-fast days, favourite fillings are shredded cooked chicken breasts or shredded cooked pork. Instead of tomato sauce, leftover sauce from Mole Poblano can be used.

Atole de Leche

MILK ATOLE

Father Sahagún recorded a great deal of information about the Aztec cuisine including the atoles or corn drinks. This is an early colonial version of the drink since the Aztecs had no cattle and therefore no milk. It remains popular throughout Mexico today. The corn (maize) flour, *masa harina*, used to make tortillas, is the thickening agent.

50g masa harina
700ml water
4cm piece cinnamon stick,
  or 1 vanilla bean
225g sugar
700ml milk

serves 4–6

1 Combine the masa harina with the water in a large saucepan, mixing thoroughly. Add the cinnamon stick or vanilla bean and cook over low heat, stirring well, until the mixture is smooth and thick. Draw off the heat, and add the sugar and milk.

2 Return to the heat and cook at a simmer, stirring, until the sugar has dissolved.

3 Discard the cinnamon stick or vanilla bean and serve hot in cups.

left Teotihuacans
Pyramid of the Sun;
Randy Faris/Corbis

TEMPORADA DE CUARESMA

LENT

During the forty days of Lent there are a number of dishes traditionally eaten on the fast days, including Caldo de Habas. Fresh lima beans make a good substitute.

left Oaxaca City Cathedral; Lonely Planet Images/Getty Images

CALDO DE HABAS

FRESH BROAD BEAN SOUP

450g broad beans, or lima beans
1 medium onion, chopped
2 garlic cloves, chopped
2 litres vegetable stock
50g lard or 4 tablespoons
   vegetable oil
350g tomatoes, peeled
   and chopped
1 tablespoon each chopped fresh
   mint and coriander leaves
225g tin cactus paddles
   (*nopalitos*) rinsed and
   chopped (optional)
salt and freshly ground
   black pepper

serves 4–6

1 In a large saucepan combine the beans, onion, garlic and vegetable stock and simmer, covered, until the vegetables are very soft. Remove the solids from the soup and purée them in a food processor or blender. Return them to the liquid.

2 In a frying pan heat the lard or vegetable oil, add the tomatoes and cook over a moderate heat until they are well blended and thick. Add to the soup with the herbs and the cactus paddles, if available. Season with salt and pepper to taste. Simmer for 2–3 minutes and serve hot in soup bowls.

EMPANADAS

LENTEN TURNOVERS

Popular in the Lenten period of abstinence from meat are empanadas with a special filling. Though fasting is no longer strictly observed these good dishes survive in the traditional kitchen.

THE PASTRY:
225g plain flour
1 teaspoon baking powder
½ teaspoon salt
175g lard, or half lard/half
  butter cut into bits
cold water

serves 8

1 Sift the flour, baking powder and salt into a large bowl. Using the fingertips rub the fat into the flour until it resembles a coarse meal. Make a fairly stiff dough with a little cold water, gather the dough into a bowl and refrigerate, covered with greaseproof paper, for 1 hour.

2 Roll out onto a lightly floured surface to 3mm thick and cut into eight 15cm circles. Set aside.

DE VIGILIA

THE FILLING:

80ml vegetable oil
350g bass
225g tomatoes, peeled
   and chopped
1 medium onion, chopped
12 pimiento-stuffed olives,
   halved
2 tablespoons capers
1 small egg beaten with
   ½ teaspoon water
salt and freshly ground
   black pepper

1 Heat half the oil in a frying pan and sauté the fish gently for about 5 minutes on each side, or until the flesh is opaque. Cool and remove all the skin and bones. Flake the fish and set aside.

2 In a food processor or blender, purée the tomatoes and onion. Heat the remaining oil in a frying pan and cook the tomato mixture until it is well blended and most of the moisture evaporated, about 10 minutes. Add the olives, capers and fish and season with salt and pepper. Spoon about 2 tablespoons of the filling across the centre of each circle of pastry, stopping short of the edges. Moisten the edges of the pastry with the egg and fold over to make a turnover, pressing the edges firmly together. Prick the tops in two or three places with the tines of a fork and brush with the egg. Bake on an ungreased baking tray in a preheated 200°C/400°F/gas 6 oven for 10 minutes, then reduce the heat to 180°C/350°F/gas 4 and bake for 30 minutes longer, or until golden brown. Serve as a first course.

CAPIROTADA

BREAD PUDDING

This very special bread pudding is a great favourite during Lent and for any vigil before a feast day in Mexico. This recipe was given to me by my husband's grandmother, Doña Carmen Sarabia de Tinoco, who was a gifted cook.

THE SYRUP:
450g brown sugar, firmly packed
5cm piece cinnamon stick
1 small white onion, pierced
  with 2 cloves
1 medium green pepper,
  deseeded and sliced
peel from 1 medium orange,
  thinly sliced

25g fresh coriander leaves,
  chopped
1 medium tomato, peeled,
  deseeded and chopped
1 litre water

serves 4–6

1 Combine all the ingredients in a large saucepan, bring to a simmer and cook, partially covered, over a low heat for 30 minutes. Cool, strain and discard the solids. Set the syrup aside.

THE PUDDING:

8 slices freshly toasted firm white
  bread cut into 1.2cm cubes
3 tart cooking apples, peeled,
  cored and thinly sliced
150g seedless raisins
100g chopped blanched almonds
225g Cheddar or Monterey Jack,
  chopped

1 Butter a 2 litre ovenproof casserole or soufflé dish and make a layer of toast cubes. Pile on layers of apples, raisins, almonds and cheese until all the ingredients are used up. Pour over the syrup and bake in a preheated oven, 180°C/350°F/gas 4, for 45 minutes or until heated through. Serve hot.

left Woman making bread; Paul Harris/Stone/Getty Images

Arroz a la Mexicana

MEXICAN-STYLE RICE

This is Mexico's most popular *sopa seca*, dry soup, that comes as a separate course after soup and before the main course at *comida*, the principal meal of the day, eaten at about 2 pm or later. It is hard to imagine a festive meal without it and it is equally suitable for vigils and feasts.

450g long-grain rice
225g tomatoes, peeled, deseeded
   and chopped
1 medium onion, chopped
2 garlic cloves, chopped
3 tablespoons vegetable oil
800ml chicken stock
2 carrots, scraped and thinly
   sliced
175g fresh raw peas or frozen
   peas, thawed
1 fresh hot green chilli, deseeded
   and chopped or more to taste
1 tablespoon chopped fresh
   coriander or flat-leaf parsley

serves 6–8

1 Wash the rice well in several changes of water and let it soak for 20 minutes. Drain thoroughly in a sieve.

2 In a blender or food processor reduce the tomatoes, onion and garlic to a purée. Heat the oil in a casserole and sauté the rice over low heat, stirring constantly until it is pale gold. Do not let it brown. Add the tomato mixture and cook, stirring from time to time, until the moisture has evaporated. Stir in the chicken stock, carrots, peas and chilli.

3 Bring to a simmer, cover and cook over very low heat until the rice is tender and the stock absorbed, about 20 minutes. Serve garnished with the coriander or parsley.

The Festive Food of Mexico

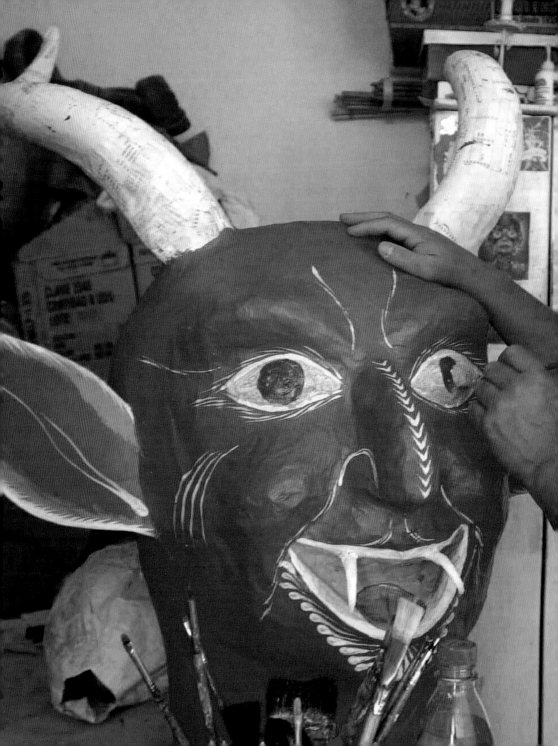

Sábado de Gloria

EASTER SATURDAY

This is the 'little resurrection' celebrated with firecrackers because Christ has risen. It is the day when Judas gets his comeuppance from the people of Mexico. Everywhere there are cardboard figures of Judas with horns and a tail, some of them gigantic, all with firecrackers attached which burn the cardboard figures when the firecrackers are lit.

The 'big resurrection' is on Sunday when Christ is in heaven completely restored and in glory, and the church is no longer in mourning with the statues of saints and the apostles covered. A favourite dish is Revoltijo, a vegetable fricassée made with a local green vegetable, *romeritos*, which looks like rosemary but has thin fleshy leaves. These have to be stripped off the woody stems before the vegetable can be cooked. Any leafy green vegetable can be used. Spinach is a good substitute. Revoltijo is accompanied by shrimp fritters. At this time of year there is bound to have been a dish of Mole Poblano (see page 66).

Traditionally the sauce accompanying the turkey is abundant and some could easily be put aside and refrigerated for other dishes, such as Revoltijo.

left Mexicans celebrate Holy Week; Susanna Gonzalez/Getty Images

Revoltijo

VEGETABLE FRICASSÉE

450g *romeritos*, or any greens
   such as spinach, cooked
   and chopped
1 x 275g tin *nopalitos* (cactus
   paddles) rinsed and
   drained, or substitute
225g French beans,
   cooked and coarsely
   chopped
6 small new potatoes, cooked,
   peeled and quartered
225g dried shrimps

3 tablespoons freshly made
   breadcrumbs
2 large eggs, lightly beaten
salt
vegetable oil
450ml Mole Poblano sauce

serves 4–8

1 On a platter assemble all the
cooked ingredients. In a saucepan
combine half the dried shrimps
with enough water to cover, bring
to a simmer and cook, uncovered,
for 20 minutes. Drain and set
aside with the cooked ingredients.

2 Clean the remaining dried
shrimps and grind them in a food
processor or blender. In a bowl
combine the ground shrimps with
the breadcrumbs and the eggs,
adding more breadcrumbs if
necessary to give the mixture
sufficient body. Season with salt,
if required.

3 In a frying pan heat the oil,
enough to reach a depth of about
2.5cm, and fry the shrimp mixture
1 tablespoon at a time until lightly
browned on both sides. Drain on
kitchen paper and keep warm.

4 In a casserole or saucepan heat
the mole sauce, add the romeritos
or other greens, cactus pieces or
French beans, potatoes and
boiled shrimps. Just before serving
add the shrimp fritters.

EASTER SUNDAY

Whatever else is on the table at *comida* on this feast day, there will be Bacalao a la Vizcaina, Salt Cod, Basque-style. It is the day when the cooking traditions of Mexico and Spain meet. There is a large Basque colony in Mexico and Basques have contributed a great deal to the country right up to the presidency. The dish has evolved in Mexico and there are many versions slightly different from each other and from the original. The original itself owes much to Mexico as it depends on Mexican peppers.

BACALAO A LA VIZCAINA

SALT COD, BASQUE-STYLE

450g dried salt cod
2 medium onions, finely chopped
3 tablespoons olive oil
3 large garlic cloves
1 slice of firm white bread,
  toasted and chopped
1 sweet red pepper, deseeded and
  chopped
900g tomatoes, peeled, deseeded
  and finely chopped
1 teaspoon sweet paprika
2 tablespoons parsley, chopped
450g potatoes, cooked and sliced
125ml dry sherry
salt and freshly ground
  black pepper

THE GARNISH:
green olives, triangles of fried
  bread and tinned pimiento
  morrón

1 Soak the cod in cold water overnight. Drain the fish and rinse it in fresh water. Put it into a saucepan with cold water to cover and one of the chopped onions. Bring to a simmer and cook over very low heat for 20 minutes or until the fish is tender. When it is cool enough to handle remove any skin and bones and cut it into 3.5cm pieces.

2 In a frying pan heat the oil and fry the garlic over low heat until brown. Remove and discard. Add the remaining onion to the pan and sauté until it is soft.

3 In a food processor or blender combine the toast, pepper, tomatoes and paprika and reduce to a purée. Add to the frying pan and cook until the mixture is thick and well blended, about 10 minutes. Add the parsley, potatoes, cod, sherry, a little of the water in which the cod was cooked, and salt and pepper to taste. Simmer over a very low heat just long enough to heat the mixture through, about 5 minutes. Garnish with the olives, fried bread and slices of pimiento.

CREME CARAMEL

A favourite Spanish dessert, this is equally popular in France and Mexico. It would be appropriate as the ending to any festive meal or any ordinary *comida* for that matter. Though it can be made in a large caramelised mould, it is much more popular to have small individual custard cups for serving.

TO CARAMELISE THE CUSTARD CUPS:
100g sugar
2 tablespoons water

serves 6

1 Have ready six custard cups warmed by standing them in hot water.

2 In a small saucepan, over a moderate heat, combine the sugar and water and cook, stirring constantly, until the sugar melts and turns a rich golden brown. Divide the caramel among the custard cups, pouring it in and turning the moulds so that the caramel covers the bottom and sides. As soon as it stops running turn the cups upside down on a flat surface.

THE CUSTARD:

1 litre milk
175g sugar
8 eggs, lightly beaten
1 teaspoon vanilla essence
pinch of salt

1 Bring the milk to scalding point in a saucepan over a moderate heat. Set aside. In a large bowl beat the sugar gradually into the eggs. Add the milk, vanilla and salt. Mix well, and strain into the caramelised custard cups.

2 Place the cups in a baking pan filled with hot water that reaches halfway up the cups and bake in a preheated oven, 180°C/350°F/gas 4, for 1 hour, or until a knife inserted into the custard comes out clean. While cooking do not let the water in the baking pan come to a boil. Lift out the custard cups and let them cool, then refrigerate.

left Stockfood
Creative/Getty Images

3 To unmould, run a wet knife between the custard and the mould, then place a plate upside down over the cup and invert it quickly.

MARGARITA

TEQUILA COCKTAIL

Though Tequila is often drunk in the traditional way with lime juice and salt, this sophisticated drink has become such a favourite that it is welcome at any time and especially when there is a fiesta. It is important to use fresh lime juice; lemon juice is a poor substitute.

cut lime
salt
3 tablespoons white tequila
1 tablespoon Cointreau or
   Triple Sec

1 tablespoon lime juice
3 or 4 ice cubes

Serves 1

Rub the rim of a cocktail glass with the cut lime, then dip the rim in salt. Combine the remaining ingredients in a mixing glass and stir well. Strain into the prepared cocktail glass.

DÍA DE LA INDEPENDENCIA

INDEPENDENCE DAY

This is a double festival, first celebrated in Puebla on St Augustine's Day, 28th August 1821. Mexico's Independence Day is 15th September. Chillies en Nogada, regarded as the national dish, was created to honour the patron saint of Augustin de Iturbide, leader of the forces that finally broke Spain's domination of Mexico. The colours are those of the Mexican flag, green, white and red. Walnuts at this time of year have been freshly harvested and are easy to peel. The nuts are soft and milky and delicately flavoured. Pomegranates, whose seeds are the red of the flag, are also in season and the leaves of flat-leaf parsley, the green of the flag, are bright and large. The peppers used are the tapering, very dark green, mild poblanos with their rich, subtle flavour. When ripe red and dried, they are the mild, equally rich-tasting ancho chillies, central to Mexican cooking.

Independence celebrations begin the night before to commemorate the moment when Father Hidalgo gave the 'Grito', the cry to overthrow Spain and liberate the country. Paradoxically he was a priest of Spanish origin. The feasting is the following day when Chillies en Nogada will be served at *comida*. Flan will almost certainly end the meal and plenty of tequila will be available. Beer, wine, pulque (a Mexican beer made from the *agave* – century plant) and probably more tequila will be served. Increasingly margaritas are the favourite way of serving tequila though the traditional lick of salt, shot of tequila and suck of a halved lime is still popular, especially among the gentlemen riders dressed in *charro* costumes – elaborate cowboy outfits with huge sombreros – who take part in rodeos on Sundays and holidays.

left Fireworks light up the sky above Mexico city; Jorge Silva/AFP/Getty Images

CHILES EN NOGADA

GREEN PEPPERS
IN FRESH WALNUT SAUCE

Poblano peppers are seldom available outside Mexico. The best substitute is large, sweet green peppers. Many cooks like to dip them in beaten egg and fry them. They are then served warm with the cold walnut sauce. Some people like a sweetish sauce flavoured with a little ground cinnamon. I prefer it slightly salty. When fresh walnuts are not available, soak ordinary walnuts overnight.

6 poblano peppers, or
  6 large sweet green
  peppers
pomegranate seeds
flat-leaf parsley

THE PICADILLO
STUFFING:
2 tablespoons olive or
  vegetable oil
900g finely chopped,
  lean, boneless pork
1 large onion, finely
  chopped
1 garlic clove, crushed
450g tomatoes, peeled,
  deseeded and chopped

2 small hot green
  chillies, deseeded and
  chopped
1 medium pear, peeled,
  cored and chopped
1 medium peach, peeled,
  pitted and chopped
2 tablespoons seedless
  raisins
2 tablespoons blanched,
  slivered almonds
salt and freshly ground
  black pepper

serves 4–6

1 Heat the oil in a large heavy frying pan and sauté the pork until it is lightly browned. Add the onion and garlic and cook until soft. Spoon off any excess fat.

2 Add the tomatoes, chillies and season to taste and cook, uncovered, over a low heat for 15 minutes. Add the fruit, raisins and almonds and cook over a low heat for a further 15 minutes. Set aside until you're ready to stuff the peppers.

TO PREPARE THE POBLANOS:

1 Impale the peppers on a large fork over a gas flame until the skin blackens and blisters. Put the pepper in a plastic bag, adding the remaining peppers as they are done. Leave for about 30 minutes then rinse off the thin papery skin.

2 Carefully slit the peppers lengthways and remove the stems, seeds and veins, taking care not to cut through. Fill the peppers with the picadillo stuffing and set them aside. Fasten them with toothpicks. The batter in which they are fried will seal them.

THE SAUCE:

100g walnuts, soaked,
  peeled, patted dry and
  ground fine
225g cream cheese, softened
225ml milk or single cream
1 tablespoon sugar (optional)
pinch of ground cinnamon
  (optional)

1 In a bowl work the walnuts into the cream cheese, then beat in enough milk or cream to make a sauce the consistency of mayonnaise. If using sugar and cinnamon add them to the sauce at this point.

FOR THE BATTER:

2 large eggs, separated
salt
flour for dusting the peppers
oil for deep-frying

1 In a bowl beat the egg yolks and add the salt. In another bowl beat the whites until they stand in firm peaks. Combine the egg yolks and whites.

2 Dust the peppers with flour then dip into the egg mixture. Fry the peppers in hot oil until they are golden brown all over.

3 Lift them out onto a serving platter and cover with the sauce. Garnish with pomegranate seeds and sprigs of flat-leaf parsley.

FRITTERS

Mexico adopted churros from Spain, making enough of a change in the ingredients to call them its own. They are named after the *churro*, a Spanish sheep with long coarse hair. Churros are sold at fairs from small portable cooking stalls called *churrerias* where they go straight from the deep-fryer to the customer. Welcome at any time, they are always found in the market at holiday times and no fiesta would be complete without them. In Mexico a cut-up lime is added to the cooking oil, giving the churros a subtly different flavour.

oil for deep-frying
1 lime, quartered
½ teaspoon salt
1 tablespoon granulated sugar
175g plain flour
2 eggs
caster sugar for dipping

makes about 12

1 Heat the oil in a deep-fat fryer and add the lime pieces.

2 In a large saucepan combine 225ml water with the salt and sugar and bring to a boil. Add the flour, all at once, and beat with a wooden spoon until smooth.

3 Tale off the heat and add the eggs, one at a time and beat until the mixture is satiny. Spoon the mixture into a piping bag fitted with a fluted 1cm nozzle. As soon as the oil reaches 190°C/ 375°F on a frying thermometer, lift out and discard the lime pieces.

4 Pipe the dough into the oil, allowing about 15cm for each churro and fry until golden, 3–4 minutes. Drain on kitchen paper and roll in caster sugar. Eat them warm.

El Platillo Nacional

THE FESTIVAL NATIONAL DISH

Mole Poblano de Guajolote, the great festive dish of Mexico, appropriate for any grand or happy occasion is served at engagement parties, weddings, christenings, birthdays, anniversaries or family gatherings for Sunday *comida* (lunch). It dates back before the conquest of the country by Spain, and reflects Mexican cuisine, based on sauces. In Nahuatl, the native language, the *mollis* (changed to moles, pronounced molays in Spanish) are innumerable. Puebla de los Angeles, capital of the state of Puebla, south of Mexico City, gives its name to the national dish and the legends surrounding its origin.

When Emperor Moctezuma entertained the Spanish conqueror Hernán Cortés, turkey mole was served. In early colonial times legend has it that the dish was invented by Sor Andrea of the Convent of Santa Rosa to honour the visiting archbishop for having a convent built for her Order. She combined the foods of Old and New Worlds and this makes some sense, but the story of Fray Pascual strains credulity. Fray Pascual was in charge of his convent's kitchens when the visiting Viceroy, Don Juan de Palafox y Mendoza, came to dine. Tidying up the kitchen, he made a pile of spices and a random wind blew them into the *cazuelas*, earthenware pots, of simmering turkey and changed them into mole. The probable truth is that Sor Andrea saved the dish from oblivion by listening to the Aztec girls who had joined the convent.

Chocolate, a royal food, was forbidden to women and all but the higher ranks of the military, clergy and merchants. The girls from the Aztec aristocracy would have known of the dish and would have passed on the recipe. Sor Andrea doubtless added her own refinements, cinnamon and cloves for native allspice for example. She has earned the gratitude of all lovers of good food.

MOLE POBLANO DE GUAJOLOTE

TURKEY IN CHILLIES AND BITTER CHOCOLATE SAUCE

6 ancho chillies
4 pasilla chillies
4 mulato chillies (specialist
   importers stock these dried
   chillies)
2.7–3.6kg turkey, cut into
   serving pieces
salt
4 tablespoons lard
2 medium onions, finely chopped
3 garlic cloves, chopped
100g blanched almonds, ground
65g seedless raisins
½ teaspoon ground cloves
½ teaspoon ground cinnamon
½ teaspoon ground coriander
   seeds
½ teaspoon anise
4 tablespoons sesame seeds
1 tablespoon chopped fresh
   coriander leaves
1 tortilla or slice of white bread,
   toasted and cut up
450g tomatoes, peeled, deseeded
   and chopped
40g bitter chocolate, broken
   into bits

serves 8–10

1 Break off the stems of the chillies and shake out the seeds. Rinse them in cold water and tear them into pieces. Put them into a bowl with warm water barely to cover and leave to soak for about 1 hour. Set aside until ready to cook.

2 Put the turkey pieces into a large casserole and add enough salted water to cover. Simmer, over low heat, until the turkey is tender, about 1 hour. Drain, reserving the stock. Dry the turkey pieces with kitchen paper.

3 Heat the lard in a large frying pan and sauté the turkey pieces, a few at a time, until they are lightly browned. Transfer to a large, heavy casserole, reserving the lard.

4 Combine the onions, garlic, almonds, raisins, cloves, cinnamon, coriander seeds, anise, half the sesame seeds, fresh coriander, tortilla or toast, chillies (drained) and the tomatoes in a food processor or blender and reduce to a coarse purée.

5 Heat the lard remaining in the frying pan, adding if necessary enough to make up the quantity to about 3 tablespoons. Add the purée and cook, stirring constantly with a wooden spoon, for about 5 minutes. Gradually pour in 1 litre of the reserved turkey stock, add the chocolate, season to taste with salt and cook, stirring, until the chocolate has melted and the sauce is smooth and quite thick.

6 Pour the sauce over the turkey and cook, covered, on a very low heat for about 30 minutes for the turkey to absorb the flavours. Arrange on a large, heated platter, sprinkle with the remaining sesame seeds and serve with hot tortillas, Frijoles (beans), Guacamole and plain white rice.

FRIJOLES

BEANS

The common bean, is always served, in its dried not fresh form, after the main course at *comida*. I use the recipe given to me by my husband's grandmother, Doña Carmelita Sarabia de Tinoco. Pinto beans were her favourite and would be served even after a main course as hearty as Mole Poblano.

450g pinto or red kidney beans
2 medium onions, finely
  chopped
2 garlic cloves, chopped
1 small hot green chilli,
  deseeded and chopped
1 bay leaf
2 tablespoons vegetable oil
125g tomatoes, peeled and
  chopped
salt

serves 6–8

1 Rinse the beans and put them into a large saucepan with cold water to cover by about 2.5cm. Add one of the onions, a clove of garlic, the chilli and the bay leaf. Cover, bring to a simmer and cook over a low heat, adding hot water as needed. As soon as the beans begin to wrinkle, about 20 minutes, add 1 tablespoon of the oil and continue to cook until the beans are tender, about 1½–2 hours according to how fresh the beans are.

2 While the beans are cooking heat the rest of the oil in a frying pan and sauté the remaining onion and garlic clove until soft. Add the tomato and cook for 3–4 minutes longer.

3 When the beans are soft scoop out half a teacupful of the beans and add them to the pan bit by bit, mashing them into the onion-tomato mixture, over a low heat, to form a fairly heavy paste. Stir this into the beans, season with salt and cook over low heat to thicken the bean liquid and blend the flavours. The finished beans should be slightly soupy. Serve in small bowls after the main course and eat with a spoon.

FRIJOLES REFRITOS

REFRIED BEANS

Used in many Mexican dishes, you cook the beans in the same way but instead of a small frying pan to sauté the onion mixture, use a large one and gradually mash all the beans and their liquid to a paste adding 1 tablespoon of lard or vegetable oil from time to time until the beans form a heavy creamy paste. They may be used as a spread or formed into a roll, sprinkled with grated cheese and stuck with triangles of crisply fried tortillas, when they are called *tostaditas*. Serve as a side dish.

GUACAMOLE

AVOCADO SAUCE/SALAD

One of the oldest of the Aztec dishes, guacamole is essential whether the meal it accompanies is festive or everyday. The tall, beautiful avocado tree, *Persea americana*, was first cultivated in Mexico about 7000 BC. Originally the dish was just plain mashed avocado, then tomato and onion were added with hot chillies and, after the Conquest, fresh coriander leaves, which the Spanish introduced. As the avocado flesh discolours very quickly, guacamole should be made at the last minute. The addition of oil and vinegar to prevent discoloration is a mistake as it robs the avocado of its true, exquisite flavour. Piled into a fresh, hot corn tortilla, it is an ideal accompaniment to Mole Poblano.

2 large ripe avocados
125g tomatoes, peeled, deseeded and chopped
½ small white onion, finely chopped
1 small fresh hot green chilli, deseeded and finely chopped
25g fresh coriander leaves, chopped
salt

serves 8–10

1 Peel and mash the avocados, preferably with a fork as the avocados should retain some texture. Fold in the rest of the ingredients and season to taste.

DÍA DE LOS MUERTOS

ALL SOULS' DAY

On 2nd November, All Souls' Day, it is traditional in Mexico to visit the graves of loved ones as a mark of both affection and respect. People take huge bunches of *zempazuchitl*, bright orange marigolds, and a special round coffee cake, Pan de Muerto (Bread of the Dead), which is decorated with a cross made of pieces of baked dough in the form of alternating teardrops and bones with a knob in the centre. This is not a sad day. It is a picnic in which the dead participate symbolically. Candy skulls are sold inscribed with the names of the picnickers. Despite the awful warning that the candy skull conveys, everything is lively and brilliant from the blue sky and yellow sun to the orange marigolds to the bright skirts, shirts and *rebozos* (shawls) worn by the members of family parties lovingly tending graves in the family plot. This is no day for mourning, it is a fiesta.

Some of the All Souls' celebrations are extremely elaborate, suggesting rites belonging to the pre-Christian faith of the region. In Janitzio, the small island in Lake Patzcuaro, Michoacan preparations begin two days before, when the men of the village go duck-hunting, using the traditional harpoon. The duck meat is cooked with a chilli sauce and used to stuff the tamales made by the women of the village. On All Souls' Eve, the women take the tamales and huge bunches of marigolds and a candle for each family member who has died. With their older children, they keep an all-night vigil at the graves, while the men keep vigil at home. The following day the family has a feast of tamales served with atole, coffee, pulque, beer, tequila and Pan de Muerto. It is believed that the dead have already feasted during the night of vigil in a mystical way.

left Day of the Dead Skeleton Figures; Danny Lehman/Corbis

PAN DE MUERTO

BREAD OF THE DEAD

2 tablespoons anise water
  (see method)
1 tablespoon active dry yeast
125ml lukewarm water
450g sifted plain flour
1 tablespoon salt
125g sugar
225g butter, melted
6 large eggs, lightly beaten
1 tablespoon orange blossom
  water
grated rind of 1 orange

serves about 12

1 For the anise water simmer 1 teaspoon of anise seeds in 3 tablespoons of water for 3–4 minutes. Cool, strain and set aside.

2 In a bowl prove the yeast with the water for 15 minutes or until foamy. Add enough flour to make a light dough. Turn it onto a lightly floured board and knead briefly. Shape the dough into a ball and place in a warm, draught-free place, covered, until doubled in size, about 1 hour.

3 Sift the remaining flour with the salt and sugar into a large bowl. Stir in the melted butter, eggs, orange blossom water, anise water and the grated orange rind, mixing thoroughly. Turn out onto a lightly floured board. Add the dough and knead the two together until satiny. Form into a ball and place, covered, in a warm, draught-free place to rise until doubled in size, about 1 1/2 hours. Shape into two round loaves, setting aside dough for decoration.

4 Place the loaves on a greased baking tray and decorate with a cross made of pieces of dough alternately shaped like bones and teardrops. Cover the loaves and stand in a warm place until it has doubled in size again.

5 Bake the loaves in a preheated oven, 190°C/375°F/gas 5, for about 30 minutes or until done. When the bread is cool, frost it and sprinkle with coloured sugar crystals. To make the frosting add sifted icing sugar to 50ml boiling water or milk until you get a spreading consistency.

CALABAZA ENMIELADA

PUMPKIN IN BROWN SUGAR SAUCE

This is a year-round dish and, though it is a dessert, it is often served for breakfast or at *merienda*, the light supper sometimes preferred as a meal to end the day after the robust *comida*. But its bright orange colour makes it a favourite for All Souls' Day. There are many versions of a pumpkin dessert; this is my favourite.

1 pumpkin, about 1.4kg,
    preferably a thin-skinned
    variety, seeds and strings
    removed
450g dark brown sugar

serves 6

1 Wipe the pumpkin over with a damp cloth and cut it into wedges. Choose a heavy saucepan or casserole into which the pumpkin can be fitted comfortably, skin-side down. Take 350g of the sugar and sprinkle it over the pumpkin wedges, dividing it evenly. Pour about 125ml water into the pan, cover and cook over very low heat, adding a little more water if necessary, until the pumpkin is tender, about 40 minutes.

2 In a small saucepan combine the rest of the sugar with 50ml water and simmer until it is thickened. Serve separately as a sauce. Serve with a glass of milk or you can pour the milk over the pumpkin instead of the sugar syrup.

right Flower and Candle Decoration for Day of the Dead; Danny Lehman/Corbis

Virgin de Guadalupe

FEAST DAY OF THE VIRGIN OF GUADALUPE

People from all over Mexico visit the shrine of the Virgin and attend services in the basilica on 12th December. The shrine, at the foot of Tepeyac hill in the town of La Villa de Guadalupe, is only 3 miles away from Mexico City's cathedral.

Before the Conquest the hill was the site of the shrine of the Aztec goddess of earth and corn, Tonantzin, virgin and mother. The first Catholic archbishop of Mexico had it and other Aztec shrines destroyed. On 9th December 1531 a convert on his way to church had a vision of the Virgin, who told him she wanted a church built on top of the previous shrine. Poor Juan Diego found it hard to convince his bishop who sent him back to find proof. On 12th December, the last time Diego saw her, she sent him to collect pink roses which he found growing among the cacti. He gathered them up in his cloak on which appeared the image of the Virgin. This convinced the bishop and the shrine and basilica were built. All round the church are stalls selling a great variety of Mexican *antojitos* (snacks), tacos, tamales and different atoles. A traditional and favourite nibble are Gorditas de la Villa. These fat little maize cakes are made from cooked, ground hominy corn but *masa harina* (flour for tortillas) can be used. Economy-minded home cooks are said to wet stale tortillas and grind them up into a dough to make Gorditas but I have never come across them and don't want to!

left Aztec dance in front of the basilica of our Lady of Guadalupe; Sergio Dorantes/Corbis

Gorbitas
de la Villa

LITTLE FAT MAIZE CAKES

450g masa barina
   (tortilla flour)
1 teaspoon baking powder
225g caster or icing sugar
225g lard or butter
6 egg yolks, lightly beaten

makes about 30

1 In a bowl, sift together the tortilla flour, baking powder and sugar. Rub in the lard or butter with the fingertips to make a coarse crumble. Stir in the egg yolks, adding a little water if necessary, to make a soft dough. Shape into little fat cakes. Traditionally the dough is pinched out to form small points round the edges. Bake on a preheated griddle for 2–3 minutes on each side, turning once. Wrap 3–4 in coloured tissue paper.

right Mennorite family harvesting field of corn; Robert Freck/Stone/Getty Images

NOCHE DE RÁBANOS

RADISH NIGHT

In Oaxaca, a state where the pre-Colombian past is very present, there is a curious festival on Christmas Eve called Noche de Rábanos. Large radishes are in season and they are carved into fancy shapes and used to decorate the market stalls and restaurants around the Plaza of Oaxaca City. The state is famous for its black and beautiful green pottery and all year long the potters save up imperfect plates and dishes. On Radish Night buñuelos are served on the pottery and when the revellers finish eating they smash the flawed plates. By midnight the square is a sea of broken crockery. The festive food is, of course, the buñuelo.

left Bunuelos; Mario Cristofori/zefa/Corbis

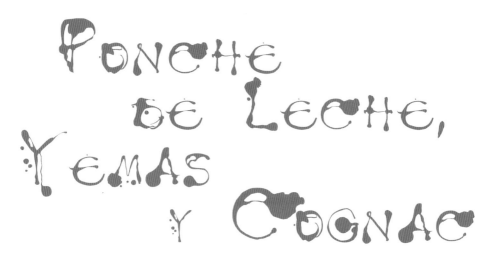

CHRISTMAS EGGNOG

A light eggnog made with milk instead of the more usual cream, it is rich and generously alcoholic without being cloying. It is a popular drink for Christmas to serve at any time with sweet cakes or cookies.

15 egg yolks
450g caster or icing sugar
2 litres milk
1 tablespoon grated orange peel
1 bottle Cognac or other brandy
ground cinnamon
cinnamon sticks

makes 4.5 litres

1 Beat the egg yolks with the sugar in a large bowl until light and lemon-coloured. Whisk in the milk. Pour the mixture into the top of a double boiler set over hot water and cook, stirring, on very low heat until the mixture is thick enough to coat the spoon. Remove from the heat and stir in the grated orange peel. Whisk in the brandy and serve warm in 125ml punch cups, topped with a little cinnamon. Serve with cinnamon sticks, if desired.

LAS FIESTAS DE NAVIDAD

CHRISTMAS

After the Posadas, re-enacting the Holy Family's search for room at an inn, Mexico celebrates with Midnight Mass followed by a veritable feast. Traditionally the meal begins with a rich chicken consommé enlivened with sherry, followed by a dried salt cod dish. The main course is stuffed roast turkey or turkey in mole sauce and Ensalada de Nochebuena.

The meal reflects the colonial influences in Mexican cooking with New and Old World foods combining: the turkey a New World bird domesticated by the Aztecs and salt cod very much a Spanish favourite, avocados and chillies indigenous foods, apples, almonds and raisins introduced. There are cakes, biscuits, nuts, fruits both fresh and dried, buñuelos and gaznates and sweetmeats to round off the feast. And to drink there is beer, wine, sparkling cider, fruit drinks and especially tequila. Children are not given their presents until January 6th, the day when the Three Kings came with their gifts for the infant Jesus.

It is the most colourful of all the fiestas, from the midnight church ablaze with light to the family table loaded with food and decorated with the scarlet brilliance of the Christmas flower, the poinsettia.

left Children sitting on a fence with a sparkler at Christmas, Michoacan; Robert van der Hilst/Stone/Getty Images

DRY SOUP FOR CHRISTMAS

The curiously named dry soup is a rice, pasta or tortilla dish that follows the *sopa aguada* (wet soup). Rice and pasta were both unknown to the Aztecs who invented the term *sopa seca* to describe the new dishes. This one is special for the festive Christmas Eve dinner.

225g thin macaroni, or use
   penne, fusilli or other pasta
1 tablespoon salt
butter for greasing baking dish
   and topping
100g mild Cheddar cheese,
   grated
2 tablespoons chopped parsley

THE BÉCHAMEL:
2 tablespoons butter
2 tablespoons flour
225ml milk
salt, freshly ground white pepper

THE TOMATO SAUCE:
1 tablespoon olive
   or vegetable oil
1 small onion, finely chopped
1 garlic clove, chopped
1 sweet red pepper, peeled,
   deseeded and chopped
450g tomatoes, peeled
   and chopped
¼ teaspoon sugar
2 teaspoons tomato purée
50ml water
salt and freshly ground
   black pepper

serves 4–6

1 Bring a large saucepan of salted water to a brisk boil. Add the pasta, stir and boil, uncovered, until the pasta is tender, about 10 minutes. Drain and set aside.

2 To make the béchamel, heat the butter in a saucepan and stir in the flour with a wooden spoon. Cook over low heat, stirring, without letting the mixture colour, for 2 minutes. Remove from the heat and gradually add the milk, stirring to mix, until the sauce is smooth. Season with salt and pepper, return to the heat and cook, stirring, over a low heat for 5 minutes. Set aside.

3 Make the tomato sauce by heating the oil in a saucepan and sauté the onion, garlic and sweet red pepper until the vegetables are soft. Add the tomatoes, salt, pepper, sugar and tomato purée, and simmer over a low heat. If the mixture is at all dry, add a little water. Continue to simmer, uncovered, until the sauce is well blended, stirring from time to time for about 15 minutes. Measure the sauce. There should be 225ml. If necessary reduce over a brisk heat or add water to make up the quantity. Press the sauce through a sieve set over a bowl, rubbing the solids through.

4 To assemble the dish, butter a 2-litre baking dish generously. Make a layer of half the pasta and top with the tomato sauce. Sprinkle with half the grated cheese and top with the rest of the pasta. Finish the dish with the béchamel sauce and the remaining cheese. Dot with butter and bake in a preheated oven, 180°C/350°F/gas 4, for 20–30 minutes or until the dish is heated through and the top lightly browned. Serve garnished with parsley.

LA NOCHEBUENA

CHRISTMAS EVE

After Midnight Mass, instead of the more traditional turkey, this is a popular dish for the Christmas Eve festive dinner.

POLLO EN SALSA DE CASTAÑAS

CHICKEN IN CHESTNUT SAUCE

1.6kg chicken, cut into
serving pieces
2 onions, chopped
bouquet garni: sprig of
thyme and marjoram and
1 bay leaf tied together
with thread
125ml dry white wine
1 litre chicken stock
salt and freshly ground black
pepper
450g whole peeled chestnuts
(tinned) or equivalent fresh
450g tomatoes, peeled and
chopped
125ml double or heavy cream
4 tablespoons medium-
dry sherry

serves 6

1 Put the chicken pieces into a heavy casserole with one of the onions, the bouquet garni, dry white wine and enough chicken stock to cover. Season to taste with salt and pepper, cover and simmer over a very low heat until the chicken is tender, about 45 minutes. Lift the chicken out to a dish, cover and keep warm. Pour the chicken stock into a bowl and skim off as much fat as possible.

2 In a food processor combine the chestnuts, tomatoes and second onion with 225ml of the stock and reduce to a purée. Transfer to a casserole and thin to a sauce consistency with as much of the remaining chicken stock as needed. Simmer, covered, over low heat to blend the flavours for 5 minutes.

3 Add the cream, sherry and chicken pieces and cook, over a very low heat, for just long enough to heat the chicken through. Serve with plenty of plain rice.

ENSALADA DE NOCHE BUENA

CHRISTMAS EVE SALAD

In the past the salad dressing was simply 100g sugar mixed with 3–4 tablespoons wine vinegar. Nowadays mayonnaise or vinaigrette (3 parts oil to 1 part vinegar, salt and pepper) are preferred. *Jícama* is a Mexican root vegetable which looks rather like a turnip and is eaten raw. The flesh is crisp and fresh-tasting. Tart cooking apples are the best substitute if *jícamas* are not available.

3 medium beetroot, cooked, peeled and coarsely chopped
3 oranges, peeled and sectioned
2 small *jícamas*, or 2 tart cooking apples, peeled, cored and chopped
2 bananas, peeled and sliced
3 slices fresh pineapple, cut into cubes
lettuce leaves
50g chopped peanuts
seeds from 1 pomegranate
125ml mayonnaise or vinaigrette
1 stick of sugar cane, peeled and chopped (optional)

serves 6–8

1 In a bowl mix together the beetroot, orange segments, *jícamas* or apples, bananas and pineapple and chill thoroughly.

2 Line a salad bowl with the lettuce leaves and pile the salad in the centre. Garnish the salad with the peanuts and pomegranate seeds. Serve the mayonnaise or vinaigrette separately. If the sugar cane is available, add it to the salad.